Dark

Winter's

Night

Struggling Through
The Pain Of Divorce

Brenda Stephens

PUBLISHED *by* PARABLES
Earthly Stories with a Heavenly Meaning

Title: Dark Winter's Night:
      Struggling Through The Pain Of Divorce
      Creator(s):Brenda Stephens

All Rights Reserved
Copyright: August, 2017 to Brenda Stephens
ISBN 978-1-945698-25-5

Published By Parables
www.PublishedByParables.com

Graphics: www.unsplash.com

Dedication

This book is dedicated to many people. Without them I would not have survived my divorces.

Kimberly Dunlap-You held me when I cried the day my second divorce was final and you were the person I called when I found out he remarried. You were my rock during that time. I love you!

Katrina Maxwell-Without you, Bestie, I might have gone on a rampage the night I found out about my third husband. But you drove an hour and a half to hold me while I cried about it. I love you!

My family at Mill Creek Foursquare Church in Mill Creek, WA.-My family could not have made it through those first months after my third divorce without you. We all love you!

My ladies Bible study at Jackson Prairie Assembly of God-You ladies helped to put me and my family back together after we moved back to Chehalis after my third divorce. We were broken and hurting and you just loved us. I love you all!

Hebrews 12: 1-2 (NIV)

Therefore, since we are surrounded by such a huge crowd of witnesses to the life of faith, let us strip off every weight that slows us down, especially the sin that so easily trips us up. And let us run with endurance the race God has set before us. We do this by keeping our eyes on Jesus, the champion who initiates and perfects our faith. Because of the joy awaiting him, had he endured the cross, disregarding its shame. Now he is seated in the place of honor beside God's throne

Faith Like Diamonds

It was a simple gold cross with diamond-like stones on it. My children gave it to me for Easter and I wore it proudly. Church was basically the same as in the past. It was Easter. Maybe it was me. I'm not sure; but, Easter services usually seem the same. This year videos of "The Passion" were shown on the screen with heart stirring music. But this year I didn't feel the life. I only felt the sorrow, encased as I was in my depression. My husband wanted to end our marriage. The love of my adult life was throwing me away, rejecting me, telling me that once again, I wasn't good enough.

As Hebrews 12:1-2 was read I followed along in my Bible. One phrase jumped out at me. Hearing it read this time was different, different from any other time in my life: He endured, because joy would be the reward, He endured. He endured and gave us eternal life.

If I could endure this trial, this tragedy -- this time -- if I could endure, it would become like one of the diamonds on my necklace. The heartbreak? I was facing another divorce! My sorrow could be turned to joy. If I endured -- my sorrow would be like diamonds on my cross.

My Prayer

Daddy, As we start this journey together, for the joy you set before us, for the diamonds on our cross, I pray for your guidance with every step. Amen

Numbers 23:19

God is not a man, so he does not lie. He is not human, so he does not change his mind. Has he ever spoken and failed to act? Has he ever promised and not carried it through?

God Doesn't Lie

God doesn't lie. Because He doesn't lie I can believe that what He says in His Word is truth. He doesn't change His mind, ever. This means I can be confident that when He makes a promise He will follow through with that promise. It may take years of waiting but what God promises will happen. In the meantime I will wait for the Lord, I will be strong and take heart and wait for the Lord.

When the Bible says to delight yourself in the Lord and He will give you the desires of your heart (Psalms 37:4) it literally means that He will do what He has promised. God is the ultimate authority on truth. He never changes His mind on the truth. Abraham waited 25 years for God's promise to be fulfilled. But what God promised did come to pass. He never lost faith. He never lost sight of the promise God made to him.

Broken promises always seemed to play a big part in my life. They started with my dad then worked their way through each of my husbands. This created an inner environment of doubt and disbelief. The result? I have a hard time believing when someone/anyone makes a promise. Lies have been a constant part of each of my marriages too. Consequently, when I hear that God is always truthful; and when I hear that God always keeps his promises – I have a hard time with that.

Yet, I keep hearing that God is always consistently truthful. And then I keep hearing that God won't break his promises! What is that? Even my earthy father broke his promises to me. In fact, he still does. So I don't have a lot of good examples of what keeping promises looks like. But I am willing to watch and learn.

My Prayer

Abba Father, I am willing to learn. I am willing to trust. I am willing to take you at your Word. I choose to believe that you do not lie. I choose to believe that you keep your promises. Your Word says that I should delight myself in you and you will give me the desires of my heart. I don't know what my heart desires right now, Lord, because you have so blessed my life these last few months. But you do. I do know, Lord, that I want complete reconciliation with my son. This is my hearts cries right now, Lord. And I'll hang on to the promises you have given me.

Psalms 81:6-7, 10c.

Now I will relieve your shoulders of its burden; I will free your hands from their heavy tasks." He said "You cried to me in trouble and I saved you ...only test me. Open your mouth wide and see if I won't fill it. You will receive every blessing you can use.

Panic

"Help me Lord," I cried.

"It is too much. I can't do this. I can't be a single parent. There is no way," my mind rebelled.

"I can't be both Mom and Dad. I can't pay all the bills, keep the house clean, buy the groceries, do laundry, maintain the car and computer, discipline the kids, help with homework, spend time with the kids, go to church, do good news club, do sleepovers and I couldn't do anything else that my mind didn't conjure up in that moment of panic. When would I have time for you, Lord, or any moment for me?

HELP, LORD! HELP!

What is this? What is this word from the Psalmist? A lifeline? A promise that says you will help? When I cry out, you will save me! Thank you, Lord. And thank you that you are a Father to my children. Help me to remember that more often.

My Prayer

Heavenly Father, I thank you that you are my helper. That you free me from my heavy tasks and lift my heavy burdens when I ask. Help me to remember that I am not doing this on my own, that you are by my side. That as long I ask for help, help will come. And you have and continue to be. Amen

Isaiah 41:10 (AMP)

'Do not fear [anything], for I am with you; Do not be afraid, for I am your God. I will strengthen you, be assured I will help you; I will certainly take hold of you with My righteous right hand [a hand of justice, of power, of victory, of salvation].'

Fear

"*I*'m scared, Lord. How am I going to do this? How am I going to get through the days and nights? How am I going to pay the bills? Buy groceries? Keep the kids happy? How am I going to raise Sam by myself? I am not a tomboy mom. I don't know anything about playing sports. How do I give him what he needs? And the girls need a dad. How am I going to DO THIS, GOD? I know I'm screaming. Can you hear me?

"Then I get your gentle answer telling me you are with me, not to fear. My divorce battered, storm weary soul finds peace. Because I know when I let go, and let you, everything is wonderfully taken care of because you promised if I would heed your call to...

*"Come to Me, all who are weary and heavily burdened
[by religious rituals that provide no peace], and I will
give you rest [refreshing your souls with salvation].
Take My yoke upon you and learn from Me [following
Me as My disciple], for I am gentle and humble in
heart, and you will find rest (renewal, blessed quiet)
for your souls. For My yoke is easy [to bear] and My
burden is light."* Mathew 11:28-30(AMP)

My Prayer

Daddy, In my fear, I turn to you. I trust you to be
there for me, to help me and guide me. Take my
burdens and give me the yoke you would have me
carry. Amen.

2nd Timothy 1:7 (amp)

For God did not give us a spirit of timidity or cowardice or fear, but [He has given us a spirit] of power and of love and of sound judgment and personal discipline [abilities that result in a calm, well-balanced mind and self-control].

Fear (Recurring)

A sink full of dirty dishes, dirty diapers, toys and clothes everywhere, and me depressed for three weeks. Not a good combination.

"Lord, is this what my life is now? Is this what the divorce has sentenced me to endure? An endless cycle of depression and guilt? And an endless mess that is never clean?"

No, because God is my Redeemer and depression is wrapped up in fear. And my Jesus has not given me a spirit of fear but of power, love, and a sound mind.

Will the pain of the divorce ever stop? Yes, because I know that "all things work together for good for those who love the Lord." (Romans 8:28) Nothing brings me greater comfort than knowing I have helped someone else get through a struggle.

Prayer

Father, I hate when fear overcomes me. In those times, you come to me and comfort my heart, reminding me fear is not from you. I get caught up in the worldly things of how much I have to do, instead of focusing on you. Help me to prioritize my time and focus on things you want me to focus on.

Hebrews 12:15(AMP)
See to it that no one falls short of God's grace; that no root of resentment springs up and causes trouble,

Bitterness

"*Do* you forgive me?"

"Of course I do. You're my husband. You came home. I love you."

On and on it went through six months of counseling. He was constantly asking for forgiveness with me constantly saying it was given or that there was nothing to forgive. Yet, I now realize that all the time I was holding a terrible root of bitterness that I couldn't see. And he wouldn't confront. I didn't see it until he walked out on us.

After he left, God showed me the bitterness I was holding in my heart and I worked on getting it out of my life. And then I could apologize to my husband. But now he was like me. Accepting, but unknowingly wrapped in a cloak of bitterness that poisons the soul.

Bitterness stole our marriage and we put it to rest on July 21, 2006. At any point God could have resurrected it, but my husbands free will left it dead. I hold on tight to Jeremiah 29:11 "For I know the plans I have for you," declares the Lord, "plans to prosper you and not to harm you, plans to give you hope and a future." (NIV)

My Prayer

Daddy, if anyone reading this has a root of bitterness they are holding onto and loving on, help them to see it and release it. Help them to pull it out and leave it with you. In Your name we pray, Amen.

Psalms 68:6

God sets the lonely in families, he leads out the prisoners with singing; but the rebellious live in a sun-scorched land.

How am I going to do this?

I was a very new, immature Christian. I hadn't grown a lot in the church I was attending. I did my best, my very best, to do all the things I knew to do. I was reading my Bible, going to church on Sunday, praying, and talking to my mom about things. But I had no idea how to do this single parenting thing -- and neither did she.

Mom had never been a single mom. She has been married to my Dad for 6 years now. I also had my best friend Russ. "Unka Russ" Meg called him. He'd been my best friend for 5 years, the best I could ask for. It didn't matter what time it was, I could call him and he would answer. He was always there for me. But, still, even he didn't know what I was enduring. He had never been married and he didn't have children.

So I started crying out to God. Daily, sometimes hourly, persistently, I cried out to God. Asking, seeking and knocking, just like the Bible said. I believed the Bible was the living, breathing Word of God and

God and everything it said was true. So I put it into practice. I cried out for a friend who knew what I was going through because my friend was going through it too. Here was someone who knew my sorrow, my struggles, my pain as a mom and my secret longings that went with being a woman.

And I cried out for God to give me strength to do the job He had called me to do. It wasn't until DeLayne (from here on out referred to as Layni) was 7 months that God brought us to a different church.

It was here, in this new church that I met so many people who poured into me. It was here I began to grow into the woman God wanted me to become. The first woman I met, who was part of the welcoming team, was Tamara. Turns out, she had been a single mom and knew my struggles. She offered to get coffee later in the week. I jumped on it. This would be the beginning of 7 of the most beautiful, wonderful, painful, stretching years I would ever know.

And God was behind every moment. Leading and guiding us all the way.

My Prayer

Daddy, For every woman who doesnt have a close friend or mentor to help them through this season, send them the very best there could be. Someone who can draw them closer to you.

Psalms 91:14-16 (NIV)

For the Lord says "Because she loves me I will rescue her: I will make her great because she trusts in my name. When she calls on me I will answer; I will be with her in trouble and rescue her and honor her. I will satisfy her with a full life and give her my salvation.

Anger

All I feel is anger. What I thought were blessings from God are always taken away. Why? What am I doing wrong? I have so many struggles in my life. All my life I have been abandoned by men. Why can't I have love? No one has ever really stayed. Why do men always walk away from me. All I want is to be loved and cherished by someone for who I am. I don't want to hide who I am or become someone else. I just want to be authentic. I want to be real. Where do I go from here? How do I ever trust again?

My Prayer

Abba, I want to be satisfied. I want to feel your blessings. I want to understand why Your blessings come so hard for me. I have nowhere to turn but to you. I can't feel your love. I ask for that right now and I ask that You fill my heart to overflowing with Your peace and love. Fill my life with the good things that come from You. Redeem what the enemy has stolen from my life. In Your precious hands, I place my life, Amen.

Hebrews 4:15 (NLT)

This High Priest of ours understands our weaknesses, for he faced all of the same testings we do, yet he did not sin.

Thrown Away

*D*amaged goods. I'm three times divorced now and that's what I see. Like a bruised melon no one wants. How is anyone going to want me after three men have thrown me away?

Is this how Jesus felt on the cross? He was rejected and thrown away by everyone. Even Peter, one of his most trusted disciples, denied even knowing him. But most hurtful had to be being rejected by God, His father. We think, how that must've hurt. But we must stop and think, His father rejected him, at the most painful point of his life. Yet, he didn't ask for any of it to stop. He completed the path set before him. His father welcomed Him home with open arms. Peter apologized, and some who had rejected him repented and accepted Him. Others didn't. Some never will.

So, in the deepest point of our rejection, we can be sure Jesus knows and shares our pain and cries with us. He had victory over rejection and so will we.

My Prayer

Jesus, You know what I'm feeling. That gut wrenching pain I feel when I think I'm going to be rejected again. Thank you for Your comfort. Thank you that I can come to You and You know what I am feeling. Please be with me and help me with my insecurities. And for those reading this let them know they are not alone. Amen

Mathew 11:30 (AMP)

"For my yoke is easy to bear, and the burden I give you is light."

Enough

When do we say enough is enough? Why do we wait so long to say I've had enough of me and all I need is You? Why don't we say at the start, "Lord, this is Your problem; have Your way with it?"

We all have our problems and we want them fixed -- our own way. For me it was my marriage. I wanted my husband to come back to me; and to God. But he didn't. That was his choice. His choices devastated me for a long time. But in the midst of the crisis I found the strength to say ENOUGH. My God knows me best and wants what is best for me.

He loves me. He was rejected for me and He held my sin and shame on the cross for me. And now He asks in return that I let Him carry my burden and I carry the one He gives me. I don't think that is a fair trade do you? His burden is so much easier than mine. And life is so much easier when we hand our problems over for him to carry and let him handle them.

My Prayer

Father, I pray for all those who are saying enough. Enough of me. Enough of my way. Enough of my situation and enough of my fixes. Enough of filling the void with things of my own choosing. Let them say "I want all of you, Jesus." Let them say, "I've had enough of my burden, would you carry it for me Jesus." Let them fill the void in their hearts with You. Bless everyone who reads these pages, Father, and let their lives be changed. Amen

Psalms 143:7-8

Come quickly, Lord, and answer me,
for my depression deepens.
Don't turn away from me,
or I will die.
Let me hear of your unfailing love each morning, for I
am trusting you.
Show me where to walk,
for I give myself to you.

Down and Out

Everywhere around me was dark, a kind of darkness that permeates everything. The kind you walk in. Wade through. But no light was strong enough to penetrate it. I could feel the hand of the Lord on me, but I was so deep in the pit that the light couldn't reach me.

My marriage is over, love is gone, I'm numb to just about everything. I want help out of this darkness. I try to climb out, but something always knocks me back, deeper into the darkness. I lose my grip and fall. Why couldn't the doctors fix me?

The sorrow and the depression was so deep, soul deep, that only God could reach me. I'd poke up my head and have a few good days, but I'd go back to my hole and my hurt and pain. In my hole I fed my hurt and pain. Until one day, after many years of being in the darkness, after years of wanting out and not knowing what to do -- I trusted God to show me what to do, and I gave myself over to Him. I asked Him what He wanted me to do. He wanted me to give Him my hurt and pain.

I didn't want to give Him my pain. I had nursed it and fed it and taken care of it for the last seven years. It was mine. He sat there, patiently waiting. Did I want to keep hurting? Or did I want to see?

I offered it up to His hands, and I saw something I couldn't see when I was curled around it. It was chained to me. But as I offered it up the locks broke, the chains fell away and I was free. Light filtered into my pit. The hurt was gone. I saw a ladder. I could get out now. I took a step forward and suddenly I was on a mountaintop, sitting beside Jesus, my head on His shoulder. In a place of freedom and joy I hadn't known in many years.

My Prayer

Father, We wander and You seek us out. We fall into a pit and sit and let it get deeper and deeper and all along you sit beside it waiting to hear us, waiting to hear the tiniest cry for help. Thank you for rescuing me, and for anyone reading this, answer their cry for help. Lift them up out of their pit. We love you Jesus, Amen

Psalms 107:9 (NIV)

For he satisfies the thirsty and fills the hungry with good things.

Longing

I have so many longings, Lord. I have longed so long for my family to be reunited. And now I long for you to bring me someone new to us now that the divorce has been finalized.

I long for my husband to come to repentance and true saving knowledge of You before it's too late. I long for my children to be happy, whole, and healed. I long for them to move past the divorce. I long for Sam to have a release from his anger.

But, mostly God, I long for more of You. I long for more intimacy with You. I am hungry for more time with you. I am hungry for your Word and time spent in prayer. You promise in your Word that as we draw near to You, You will draw near to us. Lord, I am hungry for that.

Help me to find time as a single mom to do this -- because this will heal my aching heart. You and only you can do this.

My Prayer

Lord, Sometimes our longings as single moms are greater than the time we have. But when we long for more of You, help us find the time to make it all work. Amen.

Psalms 102: 1-2 (NIV)

Hear my prayer, Lord;
let my cry for help come to you.
Do not hide your face from me
when I am in distress.
Turn your ear to me;
when I call, answer me quickly.

Rejection

Rejected. Alone. He doesn't want me. I am left alone with three kids to take care of. I wasn't good enough. All I hear is the continual voice in my head that says "if only you had been a better cook, a better mom, a better wife… If Only! If Only! If Only!"

All day long the tape plays inside my head. Lord, why do I feel this way. Why wasn't I good enough? Why couldn't I hold on to the one person who had promised to love me forever? Why didn't our vows mean anything?

And, then, your hand reached down and hits rewind on that tape and you record a new message. "I vow to never leave you or forsake you. You are my beautiful bride. I love you, no matter what you do now or tomorrow or what you did yesterday. I accept you as you are and will help you to be better. I knew you in your mothers womb and I chose you from before time. I love you."

My Prayer

Lord, These tapes we play in our head; Lord, sometimes they are awful. And dark. I ask right now, for everyone reading this, You can reach down and rewrite their tapes. Lord, give everyone reading this, give them a special new message -- just for them. Speak life and healing to their spirit. Amen

Psalms 91:14-16

"Because he loves me," says the Lord,
"I will rescue him; I will protect him,
for he acknowledges my name.
  He will call on me, and I will answer him;
  I will be with him in trouble,
   I will deliver him and honor him.
   With long life I will satisfy him
    and show him my salvation.

Rejection

I want to be satisfied, God. I want to feel your blessings, not your anger. I want to understand why your blessings always seem to be pulled out of my hands. What am I doing wrong? I have nowhere to turn but to you and I can't feel your love. All I feel is anger.

Please, God, give me back my husband. Why did you take him away? Why did you remove the blessing from my life again? I have so many struggles and there is so much that I go through. He was my bright spot.

I don't understand why. Why do all the men in my life reject me? What is wrong with me? Why can't I have love? Why can't I hold onto love? No one loves me? I can't even feel your love right now. Why can't I feel your love? Why do you always let them walk away from me?

God, all I want is to be loved for being me. All I want is to be cherished for who I am. I thought that he would finally be the one to do that. But he wasn't; and he didn't.

How do I go on from here? If you brought him back to me that would show me (and everyone else) that if I was faithful You would bless me and fill my life with good things -- and redeem what the enemy had taken from my life. But that didn't happen.

Sometimes, someone else's free will really screws up our life. And it can really mess with our head. This is where we simply must turn to God and let Him rescue us from all the confusion, doubt, insecurity and unbelief.

Where others have been faithless, He is faithful. Where others have promised love, God delivers on that promise. He will never leave us alone.

Before I found out that my third husband was molesting my girls, God made sure I had a strong support base. I was in a church I loved. I attended a Bible study and I was in a women's support group. Without those things in my life, I would have been crushed without recovery. As it was, I was shattered, but those amazing women in God's church (and some amazing women after I moved) helped me walk through the storm and rebuild.

My Prayer

Lord, I pray for the women (and men) who are on the receiving end of someone else's hurtful free will -- And, feeling awful about it. I ask that you show them it has nothing to do with them. Show them that they are precious, worthy and valuable. Show them that You have a plan and a purpose for them beyond anything they could imagine. For those who will be going through a storm in the future, I pray that You start putting the supports in place now like You did for me. Show them how much You love them. I love you, Jesus, Amen

Psalms 68:19

Blessed be the Lord, who bears our burden day by day,
The God who is our salvation! Selah.

Where are you?

"Let your character [your moral essence, your inner nature] be free from the love of money [shun greed--be financially ethical], being content with what you have; for He has said, 'I will never [under any circumstances] desert you [nor give you up nor leave you without support, nor will I in any degree leave you helpless], nor will I forsake or let you down or relax My hold on you [assuredly not]!'"

Hebrews 13:5

I'm standing here yelling in my pain: "Where are You, God? Don't You see me? Don't you care about what's going on in my life?"

Then comes the stingingly gentle reply, "I'm right here where you left me. Where, my daughter, are you?"

I looked around and I didn't recognize the terrain. It definitely wasn't where I normally warded off attacks from the enemy. I could see Father God off in the distance. In my spot. He always stood at my back. Guarding me. Protecting me.

I cried out in gut level pain, "Father, help me, forgive me of my complacency. Help me walk through the pain of this season."

In an instant, he was there, right beside me. Wrapping me in His loving arms. He filled me with the love and tenderness that can only come from Father God. I knew I was in Abba's hands and I knew without a doubt or uncertainty that He had a plan for me, and the raging storm I was in was part of that plan. I knew we would walk the road together most of the time. And, sometimes, when the road was too hard, He would lift me in his strong arms and carry me.

My Prayer

Abba, For those who need it right now, I ask you to pick them up and carry them. For, those who just need to lean on You, encourage them to lean. But, Daddy, for those like me, who go until they have to be carried, because they don't stop and rest, whisper peace. Those moments You whisper peace to me carry me so far. Help us, me and those like me – to learn to rest more. Amen.

Psalms 37:4 (AMP)

Delight yourself in the Lord, And He will give you the desires and petitions of your heart.

God's Will

Why don't you answer my prayers? Why don't I get my hearts desire? All I wanted was a happy family. Was I asking too much for You to accomplish? Was that too big of a miracle? Were my hearts desires wrong?

The answer for all of these questions was "no." But another person's free will was involved. And while God wanted to give my family our miracle, my husband refused to participate in it. He refused to bend his will to God's. He chose to let go of the blessing and let go of God. God's answer was "I can't intrude on another's free will. Let me heal. Then, when you are ready, I will bring you the desires of your heart."

Sometimes in the storm our answer seems to be the only one, so we can't see God's. God's answer is always the best when we are ready to see it.

My Prayer

Father, Help us to accept Your answer to our prayers. Whether the answer is "yes," "no," "maybe," or "I've something better in mind." Give us patience to wait on You and Your answer. Amen

Psalms 97:10-11 (AMP)

You who love the Lord, hate evil; He protects the souls of His godly ones (believers), He rescues them from the hand of the wicked. Light is sown [like seed] for the righteous and illuminates their path, And [irrepressible] joy [is spread] for the upright in heart [who delight in His favor and protection].

Suicide

Divorce is something You hate, so why am I, who loves You dearly, divorced? It makes no sense to me, Lord. Why did I have to go through this, Lord? I know that Satan has intended it for evil, but You will use it for good. You have preserved my life in the midst of this darkness. When hopelessness was my friend You came in like a thunderstorm and drove it away and preserved my life. You do this for all who put their trust in You. You shone light on my path and let me know I was not alone. You protected me when I couldn't protect myself. Forever I will love you, Lord.

You have placed me in good hands. Safe hands. And You have not forgotten me. You have returned to me the joy of my salvation. I'm forever grateful.

My Prayer

Abba, For anyone who is suicidal that is reading this I pray a hedge of protection around them right now. Send your Holy Spirit to minister life and peace. Shine Your light onto their path and fill them with hope. Let them know they are not alone. I love you, Daddy Amen

Psalms 102:28 (NIV)

*The children of your servants will live in your presence;
their descendants will be established before you.*

Father to the Fatherless

What about my kids, Lord? What about what is happening to them? They are torn apart inside. They loved their step-dad. How do I help them heal? How do I help them see that everything is going to be ok? That You are in control? That you know what You are doing and they aren't going to be let down.

How do I show them your love, Lord? I have such a big job now as a single mom to be both provider and nourisher. I don't even know if I can do that.

How do I even heal? How do I get them to admit that they are angry when I can't. We have to get there before we can move on to acceptance. Help me to help them and help me to teach them to see you not just as Almighty Father, but as Daddy

My Prayer

Father, For every parent who feels alone right now, I lift them up to you. The struggle is real, Lord, so very real – and the battle for our children is real. Sometimes, Lord, because we're single parents, things seem double hard. I pray a double blessing on every single parent, Lord. It is so hard to be mom and dad -- especially on the weekends when no one seems available to help with the kids. It's tough when you have to look after your kids 24/7 without a break. Self care goes down the drain, too. Some days it seems that all we can do is squeak out a prayer to you. We are so tired because two of the kids are sick and we're trying to make sure the third one doesn't get it. But, You intervene, You give us grace to make it and You fill in the areas we can't. Be the missing parent and spouse in every single parent's home reading this. Amen

Psalms 72:13-14 (Amp)

He will have compassion on the poor and needy, And he will save the lives of the needy. He will redeem their life from oppression and fraud and violence, And their blood will be precious in His sight.

Help

"Where is our help, Lord? I pray. I read my Bible. I go to church. I pay my tithe. I am involved in ministry. I do these things because I love You. None of what I do is done to get anything from You.

"Yet, when I read Your promises they sound hollow because I don't see them working in our lives. Why not? Why aren't You helping us? Why do I have to struggle?

"But, suddenly, You redeemed me from decades of oppression, didn't You? You erased years of negative messages in my head. I no longer hear the voices telling me I am no good. And You rescued me from a violent lifestyle when You saved me. Thank You, Lord.

"I am precious to You because no one else is like me and You love me no matter what.

My Prayer

"Father, Only You can do in a day what takes us a lifetime to do. Where we strive to fix it You take over and it's done. Help us to remember to give things over into Your hands. Amen

Psalms 81:6-7, 10(NIV)

"Now I will take the load from your shoulders; I will free your hands from their heavy tasks. You cried to me in trouble, and I saved you; I answered out of the thundercloud and tested your faith when there was no water at Meribah. Open your mouth wide, and I will fill it with good things.

Burdens

"*H*elp me, Lord. It is too much. I can't do this. I can't be a single parent. There is no way. I can't be both mom and dad. I can't pay all the bills, keep the house, buy groceries, do laundry, maintain everything, discipline the kids, spend time with friends, go to church, do sleepover's, do good news club and anything else that pops up, have time for You, and find time for me. HELP ME!

"But, wait, what is this? A lifeline. A promise that says You will help me. That You will help me when I cry out to You. Thank You. And thank You, that You are a Father to my children. Help me to remember that more often.

My Prayer

"Lord, Help us to hold onto the promises that You give us. Some times, during a divorce, the days get dark and we can't see very well. Help us to remember You are for us. And You will help us. Amen

Psalms 143:7-8 (NLT)
Come quickly, Lord, and answer me,
for my depression deepens.
Don't turn away from me,
or I will die.
Let me hear of your unfailing love
each morning,
for I am trusting you.
Show me where to walk,
for I give myself to you.

Depression

Everywhere around me was dark. It was a kind of darkness that covers everything. The kind you walk in, wade through. But no light was strong enough to penetrate it. I could feel the hand of the Lord on me but I was so deep in the pit the light wouldn't even reach me. My marriage was over, love was gone. I was numb to just about everything. I wanted help. I wanted out of the darkness.

I would try to climb out, but something always knocked me back down again. A phone call from my ex, a hug from my son, something the girls made for me and I'd lose my grip and fall. Why couldn't the doctors fix it? The sorrow and depression was so deep, soul deep, that only God was going to be able to reach me. I'd poke up my head, have a few good days, but I'd burrow back into my hole, into my hurt. In my hole I could feed my hurt and pain.

Until one day, after many years of being in the darkness, years of wanting out and not knowing what to do, I trusted God to show me what to do. I gave myself over to Him. I asked Him what He wanted me to do.

He wanted me to give Him my hurt and pain. I didn't want to give it up. I had nursed it. I had fed it and taken care of it for the last seven years. It was mine.

He sat there, patiently waiting. Did I want to keep hurting? Or did I want to see? I offered it up to Him and placed it in His hands. When I did I saw something I couldn't see when I was curled around it. It was chained to me. But as I gave it up, the lock broke, the chain fell away, and I was free. Light filtered into my pit and the hurt was gone. I saw the ladder. I could get out now. I took those steps and suddenly I was on a mountain top, sitting beside Jesus, my head on his shoulder. I was in a place of freedom and joy that I hadn't known in many years.

My Prayer

"Abba, For those suffering from this kind of deep darkness that consumes the soul, I ask for the healing and release that comes only from You.

Medicine and counseling and talking to friends are all good things to do when we feel like this. But sometimes, depression comes from a break in our soul that only God can fix.

"I ask, for those reading this, heal that break. You're gentle in Your healing and it won't hurt. But it does come with a price of giving up our right to the pain. I pray that everyone reading this will take You up on Your offer of healing. Amen

Psalms 23:4 (NLT)

Even when I walk through the darkest valley, I will not be afraid, for you are close beside me. Your rod and your staff protect and comfort me.

Trust

one. Absolutely 100% gone. Shattered. I was totally disillusioned with God, life and men. After something so devastating how on earth would I ever trust again. God could have stopped it. He could've stepped in. He could've had my girls tell me what was going on.

Those thoughts zipped through my head that cold December night as I lay in bed with a girl on either side of me. I'd been a Christian for thirteen years and had faced many fiery trials, but nothing like this.

The month before I had been informed by Child Protection Services that my husband was molesting my oldest daughter, who was approaching her thirteenth birthday. Then I found out that he had also been molesting my youngest daughter.

I never wanted another man in my life again. My trust in my husband was absolutely destroyed. I never wanted to see him again. And my trust in God? Shattered. Because I had thought I had done this relationship right. I prayed along the way, no one put up flags, the one Word I got from God was, I thought, a green light. And, this time, I had waited until our wedding night for sex, which I had never done before. So why did God let me down?

In the dark hours of the night the answers didn't come as I expected. Only the quiet assurance that He was with me, that things would be ok. We would get through this valley and come out stronger in the end.

That was December 2009. Now in May of 2017, I am stronger and closer to God than I have been in years. I trust Him with every aspect of my life. Me, my children, my grandchildren, my finances, and the most amazing fiance'. I have a kind of love I never knew could exist.

My Prayer

"Abba, You have brought me through some terrible storms in my life. But, You have never left me alone. You have walked through every one of these storms with me. For that I thank You. I know that for everyone reading this, You have done the same for them. There is a lot of brokenness in each reader, Lord, and I ask that You heal their hearts as You have done mine as they give You the pieces. Amen

Psalms 142:3 (NLT)

When I am overwhelmed, you alone know the way I should turn. Wherever I go, my enemies have set traps for me.

Overwhelmed

There was always so much to do. The house needed to be cleaned, top to bottom, every day. A though cleaning, no quick once over was good enough. Living room, kitchen, dining room, bathroom, my bedroom, and each of the children's bedroom had to be taken care of too. And then the errands, my errands; from simply dropping off library books to appointments with specialists. And then his errands that he had for me. Phone calls, drop offs, grocery runs. Whatever he didn't want to deal with I had to do. He never asked me what my day was going to be like, if I had an itinerary for the day. He just laid it all on me.

Two months into the marriage my physical body gave out from going at a pace that my body couldn't tolerate. For two years I dealt with intense pain; and, I did the best and the most that I could – but it was never enough. I was ready to be done with the marriage.

He was also very demanding of my time when he was home. And the kids? The kids had to be mini adults! They were never allowed to do anything but read after he got home.

Once he was out of the house, it was unbelievable -- I went through a day without doing anything beyond the basics. It was the best feeling I had had in two years.

God knew I was overwhelmed, He knew my physical body, and my mental well being. And God balanced the three until the time was right to free us.

My Prayer

God, For those who are overwhelmed, bring relief. Bring balance. Amen

Job 17:7 (NLT)

My eyes are swollen with weeping, and I am but a shadow of my former self.

Abuse

*M*ichael, my third husband, had been removed from the home for molesting my girls. I finally had the time to look at myself and see what my life had become since I married him. I didn't like what I saw. I was so emeshed in him. So controlled by him. I didn't know how to get myself back.

His favorite punishment for me when I didn't do what he wanted was to not talk to me for a day sometimes two. The first two weeks he was gone were weird because I didn't have a "to do" list for someone else. We didn't have to run around and make sure the house looked perfect before five, and when I say perfect, I'm not exaggerating. So many times I was told that it wasn't good enough. The stress of the last two years was gone and I was able to truly enjoy my kids again.

The abuse was so constant, so pervasive, so much a part of life that even in my relief, even when he was gone and I was glad he was gone, I still cried for him. I was still upset because what I was used to had changed and I don't do change well.

At our lowest as a family, God picked us up. Our family was a shadow of its former self, but God has brought us up and out of despair and set our feet on the highest heights.

I love the God moments in our lives. When we can look and see that something terrible happened then see that God did something better – that's a God moment.

My Prayer

Father, For the those reading this who are a mere shadow of their former selves, whose eyes are swollen from crying, be with them. Comfort their hearts. Where there has been abuse, bring healing. Where fear has control, Father, break that hold and free them. Where addiction has free reign, I bind it, and ask You to step in and clean house. In Your precious name we pray, Amen.

Job 17:11 (NLT)
My days are over. My hopes have disappeared. My heart's desires are broken.

Sorrow and Grief

My sorrow was so deep I couldn't cry. It was so deep and hurt so deep I couldn't think, couldn't feel. I was absolutely numb with shock and sorrow. I was walking through the valley of the shadow of death. I truly felt as Job did. That my days were over and my hope had disappeared. My hearts desire was broken.

My hopes and dreams for my daughter? Shattered. Meg wouldn't go to her marriage bed untouched. She was scarred. And by my then husband. I kept asking how he could do such a horrific thing.

And then the night came that I found out he had dared to do the same thing to my younger daughter. I lost it. I broke. I couldn't stay numb anymore. I cried. Oh how I cried. I cried over Meg, over Layni, over my marriage, over lost dreams, over my own stupidity. I cried in my prayer closet, at church, at Bible study. Yet, I was careful not to cry in front of Layni because she would get so upset when mommy cried.

But these tears I could not hide, stop or control.

I called my best friend who lived an hour and a half away and had been keeping very close tabs on me. She literally got in her car and came to see me. She brought the new Star trek movie and yellow roses. I tried to keep it together until she got there and we could go to my room. I managed to keep it together then I lost it again when she gave me a hug. She gave the girls instructions to watch TV and we went upstairs to my room.

She held me as I cried. It felt as if the very tears from my soul fell out, again and again and again. The pain of it; oh, the pain of it.

Meg, and Layni, and Sam not seeing his step-dad. All the pain I had been holding back came out in a rush. God had seen my dreams and hearts desires for my kids completely broken. And he brought my best friend that night to start me on the path of healing.

My Prayer

Father, For all my sisters (and brothers) reading this I ask that You bring them someone like Katrina who will help them along the path. Send someone who will help them find the path of hope and healing that takes them from death and despair, from hopelessness and brokenness and begins their journey of healing with You. Amen

Jeremiah 1:5 (NLT)
I knew you before I formed you in your mother's womb.
Before you were born I set you apart

Depression

I came across the above verse while in the midst of the darkest days of my depression over my second divorce. The depression was so dark and deep I wanted to die. Instead, God gently and slowly brought me back to life. But, I was angry, very angry about the divorce. So the depression clung to me. I got through each day with hugs from my girls, and cuddles from my son. Yet, I heard little from God during this time. Ok, I had moved a long ways away from God.

Then I found this little gem of Scripture and I clung to it. It assured me that God knew all about me. I held onto it for another reason. God knew me before I became what I called "used goods," damaged material, something someone threw away. Before I had the chance to say no, God had set me apart.

My son, yes, he would live up to his namesake, Samuel. Like the Old Testament Samuel, my Samuel had a calling. I had to move out of the darkness and step into the light of my calling too. I had to believe, really believe, that God called me; and, I had to believe that I was worthy of being called and set apart.

My Prayer

"Lord, Help me to realize that You have called me and that You have set me apart. Amen

Psalms 27:14 (NLT)

Wait patiently for the Lord. Be brave and courageous. Yes, wait patiently for the Lord.

Waiting

From the time I was sixteen this has been my life verse. I get tired of waiting and do it myself. That has gotten me two divorces because I did it my way, not waiting on God and one divorce because I didn't wait on His timing.

I didn't take David's advice to be brave and courageous -- And I messed up my life. By messing up my life I messed up my kids' life in the process. That brought on guilt. Guilt upon guilt because they didn't deserve any of it.

My second husband was a wonderful step-dad to my girls while we were married and they adored him. When he walked out on me, he also walked out on them. He didn't talk to them again until they were twelve and thirteen. He walked out when they were seven and eight.

Because of the excruciating pain of that divorce,

and having no faith in myself to raise my son alone, I married within a year of my second divorce. I didn't wait. I ended up with the wrong person. He was definitely not God's best for me. He was emotionally controlling, mentally and emotionally abusive, and he was this way with all four of us. He was also sexually molesting my daughters for two years and I had no clue. As soon as I found out he was out of the home.

But, during those very dark days, I vowed I would never marry again. And one night I sat back and cried out to my heavenly Father and said "Ok, God, I will be brave and courageous and I will wait patiently on You. I will walk where You want me to go. If you bring someone into my life great and if not great. But I will keep my eyes fixed on you."

November 3, 2014, marked the fifth year since my third husband was removed from the home. On November 8, I started a relationship with the one God picked out for me. We are getting married July 8, 2017. In the waiting I 1) waited on God 2) worked on me 3) worked on my family.

Guilt doesn't come from God. If you are feeling guilty know that God doesn't condemn you, Satan does. The next devotion is devoted to this.

My Prayer

"Daddy, I pray for all my sisters (and brothers), who, like me, made bad choices. When it came to picking men, I picked broken men. Heal that in them like you did me. Help them to take David's advice to be brave and courageous, to wait patiently on You. Help them to know, like I have found out, that You have perfect timing. And if they are patient, and wait on You, they will be greatly rewarded. Lord, I thank You for all my blessings and I thank You that You are going to bless everyone who is praying this prayer. In Jesus name I pray, Amen

Romans 8:1 (NLT)
"So now there is no condemnation for those who belong to Christ Jesus."

Guilt

The guilt. It's the one thing in all of this I couldn't handle. The guilt of what the divorce is doing to the kids and my ex doesn't even care. He never calls to talk to the girls. We were raising them together as if they were both of ours since their real dad wasn't around much. Layni thought he was her real dad for goodness sake. And he wouldn't even talk to them. It broke my heart. And I felt a tremendous load of guilt. I brought him into their lives. That guilt never totally went away.

Fast forward four years.

The new guilt was crushing me. I brought this new monster into their lives. I did this. Me. I was so desperate for a husband. God, crush me with rocks and take my life because I can't take the pain of knowing how I've allowed my children to be hurt. My daughters have been sexually molested by their step-dad for two years and I had no idea. Neither girl told me. Meg finally told a friend, whose mom spoke out.

Getting him prosecuted was the longest year of my life. I was full of guilt and didn't know how to lose the guilt. People from church, home group, friends of mine, and moms group all prayed for me.

Consciously I knew none of these things were my fault. Both of these men had free will. With that free will they had chosen to spit in God's face and on the marvelous gift He had given them. -- me and the kids. Spit in His face.

Then, God sent someone into my life for a brief season who taught me about judgment and condemnation. Condemnation is just a harsher form of judgment but it's aimed at yourself. And you're saying over and over in your head: "Your going to hell." And if, God says there is none of that for His children, we better not be pouring it out on any of His children. Especially ourselves! Guilt is the highest form of self-condemnation and never comes from God. Conviction does and with it a feeling of remorse, but once we repent the feeling is gone.

I no longer live in a place of guilt and condemnation. I gave it to God and let Him free me from those chains.

My Prayer

Abba, For all of those reading this that are bound by chains of condemnation I ask that You break them. Lead them to a place of freedom and grace. I love you, Jesus.

Psalms 138:3 (NLT)

As soon as I pray, you answer me; you encourage me by giving me strength.

Rebellion

"Why would you listen to me when You tried to warn me and I wouldn't listen? I wouldn't listen to You, but I had the audacity to think you would listen to me? You gave me very clear signs that I wasn't to marry him. I did it anyway. My way is best right?"

It's what we think. It's our attitude with God. He has to do and be whatever He says. Or our interpretation of what He said. That's the moment I speak, I pray, He should be answering me. That the way we act sometimes.

My Prayer

"Lord, You told me clearly not to get into this mess, but I did anyway. Now, because of your love for me, can you get me out? Amen

Numbers 23: 19 (NIV)

God is not a man, so he does not lie. He is not human, so he does not change his mind. Has he ever spoken and failed to act? Has he ever promised and not carried it through?

Broken Promises

From my childhood until my third husband left, men didn't keep their promises to me. The level of broken promises in my second marriage was almost unbearable. I couldn't trust anything my husband said. It got to the point that I wanted him to put any agreement in writing. Why? Because when it came time for him to fulfill his part of the deal, like staying in Washington with me and the kids, he would say that wasn't what he agreed to and my heart would break.

The pain that would pierce my heart was intense because I couldn't trust the one person on earth I loved the most. It was a long time before I tried to trust again. Unfortunately, my third husband was a casualty of my lack of trust because I never did trust him the way a wife should.

This may be an area where you struggled within your marriage. Confess it to God, then let it go. If you broke the promises, and you are still on speaking terms with your former spouse, take responsibility for your actions, and apologize – ask for forgiveness. It will mean so much to him/her. But, if you are the one whose heart was broken time after time until there was no trust left for your spouse, or for God, ask God to forgive you first for any bitterness, resentment, or unforgiveness you are holding in your heart. Give it to God everyday until you feel freedom from it. Also, realize God has never let you down. He is the only one you can trust 100%. I lost sight of that and it took me awhile to get my perspective back.

As today's Scripture says, God is not a man that He should lie. He never makes a promise and then fails to fulfill it. If it's in the Bible you can stand on it as truth. He doesn't change His mind, so I can say this: "When He makes a promise He will follow through on it."

So when it says trust in the Lord with all your heart, it is safe to do that. And as we do that, just that one simple act of obedience, of complete trust, child like trust, He will pour out blessing on your life.

Dark Winter's Night

My Prayer

"Lord, I am willing to learn. I am willing to take you at your Word. You don't lie and You keep Your promises. Where I have broken another's trust I ask for forgiveness. And wherever possible help me to ask for forgiveness. Where my trust has been broken, Abba, I give it all to You. All the anger, resentment, unforgiveness and bitterness I may be harboring in my heart, I give into Your hands. I realize that You, God, have never let me down and I have transferred my emotions from dependence on people to dependence on You. Help me not to do that. Keep watch over everyone saying this prayer today, and watch over their families. I love you so much, Jesus. Amen

Psalms 126:4 (NLT)

Restore our fortunes, Lord, as streams renew the desert. Those who plant in tears will harvest with shouts of joy. They weep as they go to plant their seed, but they sing as they return with the harvest.

Tears

I cried buckets during the marriage and rivers during the divorce. I could say that about all my marriages. Marriage was not the thing I had always been told it was. A blessed union. Full of love. Meant to be. Happily ever after.

Since my oldest sisters wedding when I was four, I had dreamed of my wedding. I dreamed of being married and raising a family together. Those dreams were crushed by my first husband. I went into that marriage a naive young girl and walked out a battered, knowledgeable woman.

I didn't get my happily ever after, or my meant to be. I got tears and pain and nights on the couch crying. When we would fight I'd cry all the more for the loss of my dreams.

My Prayer

"Lord, For those who, like me, had their dreams of happily ever after shattered, comfort them. For the tears they have cried, hold them. For the sorrow they feel, lift them up. Be their everything. Amen

Psalms 51:17 (NLT)
The sacrifice you desire is a broken spirit. You will not reject a broken and repentant heart, O God.

Brokenness

My life was shattered. I was completely broken. It had only been four months since the divorce and he was telling me he was remarried.

Wait. What was that about ten days after the divorce? Well, no wonder he pushed so hard for the divorce. My heart was in a million pieces.

I don't remember getting the kids in the car and driving home that night. I functioned on auto pilot the next morning, getting the girls ready for school and taking my son back to see his dad. Sitting in the restaurant across from the man I still so desperately loved, with our son between us, was the hardest thing I've ever done.

I wanted to yell and scream at him, "how dare you do this to us! How dare you cheat!" But I kept silent. I talked about the things our son enjoyed. I wanted to lash out and hit him with my balled fists. I wanted to beat his chest. Instead I brushed the hair out of our son's eyes and dropped a kiss on his forehead.

I haven't seen my son's dad since that meeting. We talk on the phone and that's it.

My brokenness was complete. It led to 8 years of being in and out of bed, off and on, with severe attacks of depression and a failed marriage that hurt my children and left deep, deep scars.

The brokenness was so complete I couldn't see how broken I really was. I tried dozens of ways to fix it. I failed to try the only sure way that will always heal a broken and contrite heart – Jesus!

Eight years after our divorce was final I went and kneeled at the cross. I gave Jesus all my broken pieces, not just a few, but all – including the hidden things of my heart. Gradually, Jesus healed and put the pieces together, one piece at a time, over the years. I'm a work in progress, still broken, yet healed. I offer it all to Him.

In November of 2014, a friend from high school and I started dating. He's the love of my life; the one who loves me no matter what. He's the only man in my life who has ever shown me that level of love. Jesus took me from brokenness to blessedness when I gave Him all the pieces.

My Prayer

Abba, Broken beyond belief is never a place we want to be. But it is a place You can always use if we allow it. You will take our brokenness and turn it into wholeness and use it for Your glory. And in our brokenness You pour out Your mercy and grace. You don't condemn us for being broken but love us more because we have brought our brokenness to You. We love You so much, Daddy, Amen

Psalms 56:8 (NLT)

You keep track of all my sorrows. You have collected all my tears in your bottle. You have recorded each one in your book.

Sorrow

How can one heart be so sad? How can it bear the weight of such sorrow? How much can you miss one person? How long until the pain of missing them lessens?

No, not my third husband. I was happy he was gone. Our lives were so much less stressful, my kids had a freedom they hadn't known in two years. They could laugh and joke and play and just be kids again. They could make a mess with their toys after five and no one was going to care as long as it was cleaned up by bedtime. We had cable TV and watched movies and played video games. We ate popcorn in the living room without a blanket down. (Had hardwood floors)

No, my sorrow was, in spite of our freedom, one child was missing. My oldest child had chosen to live in Arizona with my sister instead of me. And I had to let her go because of CPS's involvement in our life.

She didn't want to talk to me. But I spoke to my niece or sister about her almost daily. I loved her from a distance and prayed for her constantly. It was the only way she would let me love her.

At night, when the other two kids where asleep, I would cry out to Jesus and beg him to bring the missing piece of my heart home. Often I would feel gentle arms pick me up and surround me as my Jesus held me close to His heart and assured me that He loved me. That He "collected my tears in a bottle"

He assured me she would be home soon. And, bless the Lord, she was only gone a total of four months. We have a wonderful relationship today and she has given me two beautiful, amazing grand kids.

My Prayer

"Father, I pray for the mothers (and fathers) who have a difficult relationship with their sons and daughters. You know it is not an easy road. You took my walk with Meg from frigid to fiery. But it was a process. I ask you do the same for those who are reading this. Help them walk through the process. Help them to not lose heart in the process but to trust You. Help each one to give the process over to Your hands. For the miracle You are going to do for everyone of them I thank you. Amen

The First Step

The first step to find freedom and release is to turn your will and life over to Jesus by inviting Him into your life. Do pray the following prayer. It's your first step...

Dear Father –

I know you see my whole life. You see the good things I've done and the good things I've attempted to do. You see the mistakes I've made and the mistakes I've avoided...and, you see my sin.

I ask you to forgive me for all of my sins. Cleanse me. Make me whole. Please, come into my heart and into my life.

And, if I should stumble and fall, pick me up, dust me off, and show me your better way.

Heal me, may your grace and generosity overshadow me as I walk in the newness of life that only you can provide. I ask pray this prayer in the name of Jesus. Amen.

A Little About Me

I was married the first time when I was 21. He was a violent, angry man I left after two years and two kids. I was single four years when I met my second husband. It was a whirlwind romance and we were married in less than three months. I don't recommend anyone do this. We lasted three years before he couldn't live with my bitterness anymore. Less than a year after the divorce was final I was married again to a man who was abusive and controlling and who molested my girls.

Now, seven years later, I am engaged to an amazing, God-fearing man, who loves me for me, not for who he can make me into. I am scared but excited to start this journey.

May God bless you as richly as He has me.

Brenda Stephens

PUBLISHED by PARABLES
Earthly Stories with a Heavenly Meaning

Printed in the USA
CPSIA information can be obtained
at www.ICGtesting.com
LVHW091429260424
778544LV00036B/668